DUBROVNIK TRAVEL GUIDE 2024 UPDATED

Comprehensive Handbook for Exploring Croatia's Gem, Navigate the Cobblestone Streets, Hidden Gems, and Must-See Attractions, and local delights

Brody Valentine

Copyright ©2024 Brody Valentine

All rights reserved.

No part of this publication may be reproduced, distributed, or transmitted in any form or by any means, including photocopying, recording, or other electronic or mechanical methods, without the prior written permission of the publisher, except in the case of brief quotations embodied in critical reviews and certain other noncommercial uses permitted by copyright law

DUBROVNIK TRAVEL GUIDE 2024 UPDATED

WELCOME TO DUBROVNIK

HISTORY

WHY YOU SHOULD VISIT DUBROVNIK

WHAT TO PACK

VISA AND ENTRY REQUIREMENT

NEIGHBORHOODS AND DISTRICTS

    DUBROVNIK OLD TOWN:
    PLOČE:
    PILE:
    LAPAD:
    GRUŽ:
    BABIN KUK:
    MOKOŠICA:

GETTING THERE AND MOVING DUBROVNIK

WHERE TO EAT IN DUBROVNIK

TOP CUISINE TO TRY OUT IN DUBROVNIK

TOP ATTRACTIONS

TOP ACCOMMODATION

SHOPPING AND SOUVENIRS IN DUBROVNIK

VIBRANT NIGHTLIFE OF ARGENTINA

10 AMAZING ITENERARIES

- History Buff's Delight:
- Foodie Adventure
- Island Explorer:
- Adventure Seeker's Paradise:
- Art and Culture Trail:
- Wellness Retreat:
- Family Fun Day:
- Romantic Rendezvous:
- Nightlife Extravaganza:
- Nature Lover's Paradise:

48 HOURS IN DUBROVNIK WHAT TO EAT AND DRINK

FESTIVAL AND EVENTS IN DUBROVNIK

IDEAL VISITING TIME

VOCABULARY AND COMMON PHRASE

DUBROVNIK TRAVEL PRACTICALITIES

CONCLUSION

WELCOME TO DUBROVNIK

Welcome to Dubrovnik, a jewel of the Adriatic coast renowned for its stunning beauty, rich history, and captivating charm! Have you ever wondered why Dubrovnik is often referred to as the "Pearl of the Adriatic"? Well, it's not just for its breathtaking medieval architecture and crystal-clear waters; it's also because of its remarkable centuries-old city walls, which encircle the UNESCO World Heritage Site of Dubrovnik Old Town, offering unparalleled views of the city's red-roofed buildings and the shimmering Adriatic Sea. But Dubrovnik is much more than just a picturesque coastal town—it's a destination steeped in history, culture, and natural splendor, ready to enchant and inspire all who visit. So, are you ready to embark on a journey through the timeless beauty and rich heritage of Dubrovnik? Let's delve into this enchanting city and discover its many wonders together!

As you step foot into Dubrovnik, you'll find yourself transported back in time to a world where ancient stone walls whisper tales of centuries past. Founded in the 7th century, Dubrovnik flourished as a maritime republic known as the Republic of Ragusa, becoming a powerful force in the Mediterranean trade network. Its strategic location at the crossroads of East and West enabled Dubrovnik to prosper as a hub of commerce, culture, and diplomacy.

Throughout its storied history, Dubrovnik faced numerous challenges, including invasions, earthquakes, and sieges. Yet, through resilience and determination, the city rose from the ashes time and time again, emerging stronger and more vibrant than ever. Today, Dubrovnik stands as a testament to the enduring spirit of its people and the indomitable resilience of the human spirit.

One of the most iconic features of Dubrovnik is its imposing city walls, which stretch for over 1,900 meters and encircle the Old Town like a protective embrace. Dating back to the 13th century, these majestic walls are among the best-preserved fortifications in the world and offer panoramic views of the cityscape and the Adriatic beyond. Walking along the ramparts, you'll encounter ancient towers, bastions, and gates, each bearing witness to Dubrovnik's tumultuous past and remarkable survival.

As you explore the cobblestone streets and narrow alleys of Dubrovnik's Old Town, you'll be transported back in time to an era of knights and nobles, merchants and artisans. Admire the exquisite architecture of the Rector's Palace, the Cathedral of the Assumption, and the Franciscan Monastery, each a masterpiece of Renaissance and Baroque design. Lose yourself in the labyrinthine lanes of the Stradun, the city's main thoroughfare, where bustling markets, charming cafes, and hidden courtyards await around every corner.

But Dubrovnik's allure extends far beyond its historic walls. Venture outside the city to discover the breathtaking natural beauty of the surrounding area, from pristine beaches and secluded coves to lush forests and picturesque islands. Cruise along the coastline aboard a traditional wooden boat, explore hidden caves and grottoes, or simply soak up the sun on the sun-kissed shores of the Adriatic.

As night falls, Dubrovnik transforms into a magical wonderland, with the glow of lanterns casting a warm, inviting light over the city streets. Dine al fresco at a charming seaside restaurant, savoring fresh seafood and local delicacies as the stars twinkle overhead. Then, stroll along the waterfront promenade, where live music fills the air and the sound of laughter echoes through the night.

Whether you're drawn to Dubrovnik's rich history, stunning architecture, or breathtaking natural beauty, one thing is certain: this enchanting city will capture your heart and leave you longing to return again and again.

HISTORY

Dubrovnik, often referred to as the "Pearl of the Adriatic," boasts a rich and storied history that spans over a millennium. Founded in the 7th century by refugees fleeing the destruction of the nearby Roman city of Epidaurum, Dubrovnik grew into a powerful maritime republic known as the Republic of Ragusa. Its strategic location along the Adriatic coast made it a crucial hub for trade between East and West, leading to immense prosperity and cultural exchange.

In the Middle Ages, Dubrovnik flourished as a center of commerce, diplomacy, and art. Its skilled diplomats forged alliances with neighboring city-states and empires, ensuring the republic's independence and security. Meanwhile, Dubrovnik's artists and scholars contributed to the cultural renaissance of Europe, producing masterpieces of literature, architecture, and painting that still captivate visitors today.

The city's golden age reached its peak in the 15th and 16th centuries, when Dubrovnik emerged as a dominant force in Mediterranean trade. Its merchant fleet sailed to ports across the Adriatic, Aegean, and Black Seas, trading in goods such as salt, wine, and textiles. Dubrovnik's prosperity was reflected in its impressive architecture, with grand palaces, churches, and fortifications adorning the cityscape.

However, Dubrovnik's prosperity also attracted the envy of its neighbors, leading to conflicts and sieges throughout its history. In 1667, a devastating earthquake struck the city, causing widespread destruction and loss of life. Yet, Dubrovnik's resilience shone through as the city rebuilt and restored its damaged landmarks, preserving its cultural heritage for future generations.

In the 19th century, Dubrovnik became part of the Austro-Hungarian Empire, marking the end of its centuries-long independence. Despite this change in political status, the city continued to thrive as a cultural and economic center, attracting artists, intellectuals, and travelers from around the world.

In the 20th century, Dubrovnik faced new challenges as it navigated the tumultuous events of World War I and II, as well as the breakup of Yugoslavia in the 1990s. During the Croatian War of Independence, Dubrovnik came under siege by Serbian forces, resulting in significant damage to its historic landmarks. However, thanks to extensive restoration efforts and international support, Dubrovnik was able to rebuild and reclaim its status as one of Europe's most beloved destinations.

WHY YOU SHOULD VISIT DUBROVNIK

Buckle up and get ready for a journey through the enchanting city of Dubrovnik! Picture this: you're strolling through ancient streets where history whispers from every stone, the sun dances on the Adriatic Sea, and the scent of Mediterranean cuisine lures you around every corner. Here's why you absolutely, positively need to add Dubrovnik to your travel bucket list:

1. **Medieval Marvels**: Dubrovnik is like stepping into a real-life Game of Thrones set, minus the dragons (unfortunately). Its iconic Old Town is a UNESCO World Heritage Site, boasting majestic medieval walls that encircle the city like a protective embrace. Take a leisurely walk along these walls and soak in breathtaking panoramic views of terracotta rooftops, shimmering sea, and rugged cliffs. You'll feel like you've been transported back in time to an era of knights, kings, and epic adventures.

2. **Sun-soaked Splendor**: If you're a sun worshipper (or even if you're not), Dubrovnik's coastline will leave you utterly spellbound. With its crystal-clear waters and rocky coves, the Adriatic Sea beckons you for a refreshing dip or a leisurely kayak excursion. Find your own private slice of paradise on one

of Dubrovnik's pristine beaches, where you can bask in the warm Mediterranean sun and work on your golden tan.

3. **Culinary Delights**: Prepare your taste buds for a culinary journey like no other. Dubrovnik's food scene is a delightful fusion of Mediterranean flavors, with influences from Italy, Greece, and the Balkans. Indulge in fresh seafood caught that very morning, savory Dalmatian prosciutto, creamy Pag cheese, and mouthwatering seafood risotto. Wash it all down with a glass of locally-produced wine or rakija (traditional fruit brandy), and you'll be in foodie heaven.

4. **Culture Galore**: Dubrovnik is a cultural gem waiting to be discovered. From its rich history to its vibrant arts scene, there's something to captivate every visitor. Explore the city's numerous museums, galleries, and theaters, where you can immerse yourself in centuries of artistic and cultural heritage. Don't miss the chance to attend a performance at the historic Dubrovnik Summer Festival, where the streets come alive with music, dance, and theatrical performances against the backdrop of ancient architecture.

5. **Adventure Awaits**: For thrill-seekers and nature lovers, Dubrovnik offers a playground of outdoor adventures. Hike to the top of

Mount Srđ for jaw-dropping panoramic views, or venture into the nearby Konavle Valley for a day of cycling through picturesque vineyards and olive groves. For the ultimate adrenaline rush, why not try cliff diving or sea kayaking along the rugged coastline? Whatever your adventure style, Dubrovnik has got you covered.

WHAT TO PACK

Let's pack our bags for a trip to Dubrovnik! But hold on tight, because we're not just talking about any old packing list – we're talking about the essentials for a memorable and oh-so-stylish adventure in this Croatian gem.

First things first: sun protection is non-negotiable. The Adriatic sun can be fierce, so pack your trendiest pair of sunglasses, a wide-brimmed hat, and don't forget that trusty bottle of sunscreen. You'll thank me later when you're lounging on the beach without a care in the world.

Next up, let's talk about wardrobe essentials. Dubrovnik is all about laid-back Mediterranean vibes, so think breezy sundresses, flowy skirts, and lightweight tops in vibrant colors and fun prints. Oh, and don't forget to throw in a swimsuit or two – you'll need it for those impromptu dips in the crystal-clear waters of the Adriatic Sea.

Now, onto footwear. While those designer heels might look fabulous, they're not exactly practical for navigating Dubrovnik's cobblestone streets. Opt for comfortable walking shoes or sandals that can take you from sightseeing in the Old Town to sunset cocktails by the sea with ease.

Of course, no trip to Dubrovnik would be complete without a camera to capture all those Insta-worthy moments. Whether you're snapping selfies atop the city walls or capturing the stunning sunset over the Adriatic, you'll want to document every magical moment of your Dubrovnik adventure.

VISA AND ENTRY REQUIREMENT

Let's talk about visas and entry requirements for your epic journey to Dubrovnik! But don't worry, this won't be your typical snooze-fest of bureaucratic jargon. We're going to make this as fun and breezy as a day at the beach in the Adriatic sun.

So here's the deal: if you're a citizen of the European Union or the Schengen Area, congratulations – you're in luck! You can waltz right into Dubrovnik without so much as a second glance from immigration. Consider it your VIP pass to paradise.

But what if you're not a lucky EU or Schengen citizen? Fear not, intrepid traveler! Obtaining a visa for your Dubrovnik adventure is easier than you might think. Most visitors from non-EU countries are granted visa-free entry for short stays of up to 90 days within a 180-day period. That means you'll have plenty of time to explore Dubrovnik's medieval streets, lounge on its sun-kissed beaches, and indulge in its mouthwatering cuisine without having to worry about pesky visa restrictions.

Now, I know what you're thinking: "But what about all the paperwork? The forms? The bureaucracy?" Well, my friend, I'm here to tell you that getting a visa for Croatia is about as complicated as ordering a scoop of gelato – and just as delicious! In most cases, all you'll need is a valid passport with at least six months of validity remaining, proof of sufficient funds to cover your stay, and a return ticket to show you're not planning on becoming a permanent resident of this slice of paradise (although, who could blame you if you did?).

And the best part? Once you've got all your paperwork in order, you'll be free to embark on your Dubrovnik adventure with nothing standing in your way. So pack your bags, grab your passport, and get ready to experience the magic of Dubrovnik – because with visa requirements this easy, there's no excuse not to join the party!

NEIGHBORHOODS AND DISTRICTS

DUBROVNIK OLD TOWN:

Dubrovnik Old Town is a captivating blend of medieval architecture, cultural heritage, and timeless beauty. Wander through its ancient streets, where every corner holds a story waiting to be discovered. Marvel at iconic landmarks like the majestic Rector's Palace, the ornate Church of St. Blaise, and the imposing City Walls that have stood for centuries, offering panoramic views of the shimmering Adriatic Sea. Lose yourself in the maze of cobblestone alleys lined with charming cafes, boutiques, and artisan shops, where you can taste local delicacies, shop for handmade souvenirs, and mingle with friendly locals. From the bustling main thoroughfare of Stradun to hidden gems like the Dominican Monastery and the Jewish Synagogue, Dubrovnik Old Town is a living museum waiting to be explored.

What to Do and See

1. Walk the City Walls:

- Start your exploration by walking along the iconic Dubrovnik City Walls, which offer panoramic views of the Old Town, the Adriatic Sea, and the surrounding islands. Marvel at the historic fortifications, watchtowers, and cannon emplacements as you stroll along the 2-kilometer-long walls that encircle the city.

2. Visit Stradun (Placa):

- Take a leisurely stroll down Stradun, also known as Placa, the main thoroughfare of Dubrovnik Old Town. Lined with elegant palaces, shops, cafes, and restaurants, Stradun is the perfect place to soak up the ambiance of the city and do some people-watching.

3. Explore the Sights:

- Discover Dubrovnik's rich history and culture by exploring its many historic sights, including the Rector's Palace, the Dubrovnik Cathedral, and the Church of St. Blaise. Admire the stunning architecture, intricate stone carvings, and beautiful artwork that adorn these iconic landmarks.

4. Visit Onofrio's Fountain:

- Make a stop at Onofrio's Fountain, one of Dubrovnik's most recognizable landmarks. Built in the 15th century, this impressive fountain provided the city with fresh water from a nearby spring. Marvel at its beautiful dome-shaped structure and intricate stone carvings.

5. Discover Dubrovnik's Museums:

- Immerse yourself in Dubrovnik's history and culture by visiting its museums. Don't miss the Dubrovnik Museum housed in the Rector's Palace, which showcases the city's rich heritage through artifacts, paintings, and historical exhibits. You can also explore the Maritime Museum and the Ethnographic Museum to learn more about Dubrovnik's seafaring traditions and local customs.

6. Relax in Luža Square:

- Take a break from sightseeing and relax in Luža Square, the bustling heart of Dubrovnik Old Town. Situated just off Stradun, this lively square is surrounded by historic buildings and outdoor cafes, making it the perfect spot to unwind and watch the world go by.

7. Climb the Bell Tower:

- Ascend the stairs of the Bell Tower for stunning panoramic views of Dubrovnik Old Town and the surrounding area. Marvel at the red-tiled rooftops, ancient city walls, and sparkling Adriatic Sea stretching out before you as you reach the top of this iconic landmark.

8. Visit the Old Port:

- Wander down to the Old Port, where you can admire the traditional wooden boats and fishing vessels bobbing in the harbor. Take a leisurely stroll along the waterfront promenade, lined with seafood restaurants and cafes, and soak up the maritime atmosphere of this historic port.

PLOČE:

As you pass through the Ploče Gate, you'll be greeted by sweeping vistas of the Adriatic Sea and the rugged coastline, setting the stage for an unforgettable journey. Explore the tranquil parks and gardens that dot the neighborhood, where you can escape the hustle and bustle of the city and reconnect with nature. Take a leisurely stroll along the waterfront promenade, where you can soak up the sun, admire the yachts bobbing in the harbor, and watch the boats sail by. Don't miss the opportunity to visit the Museum of Modern Art Dubrovnik, home to a diverse collection of contemporary Croatian art, or to indulge in a refreshing swim at Banje Beach, one of the most popular beaches in Dubrovnik.

What to Do and See

1. Banje Beach:

- Start your exploration of Ploče with a visit to Banje Beach, one of the most popular and picturesque beaches in Dubrovnik. With its crystal-clear waters, fine pebble beach, and stunning views of the Old Town and Lokrum

Island, Banje Beach is the perfect place to soak up the sun, swim in the sea, and enjoy water sports like jet skiing and parasailing.

2. Dubrovnik Cable Car:

- Take a ride on the Dubrovnik Cable Car for breathtaking panoramic views of Dubrovnik and the surrounding area. The cable car station is located in Ploče, near the Old Town, and offers a scenic journey to the top of Srd Hill, where you can enjoy stunning vistas of the city, the Adriatic Sea, and the nearby islands.

3. Revelin Fortress:

- Explore the historic Revelin Fortress, a 16th-century defensive fortification located at the eastern entrance of the Old Town. Built to protect the city from potential invaders, Revelin Fortress now houses cultural events, exhibitions, and concerts throughout the year. Take a guided tour of the fortress to learn about its fascinating history and enjoy panoramic views from its ramparts.

4. Lazareti:

- Visit Lazareti, a historic complex of quarantine buildings located near Banje Beach. Built in the 17th century to quarantine travelers and goods arriving by sea, Lazareti now serves as a cultural center and event space, hosting art exhibitions, music performances, and other cultural events. Explore the atmospheric stone buildings and soak up the creative energy of this unique cultural hub.

5. Eastwest Beach Club:

- Relax and unwind at Eastwest Beach Club, a stylish beach club located on Banje Beach. Lounge on sunbeds overlooking the sea, sip cocktails at the beach bar, and enjoy delicious Mediterranean cuisine at the club's restaurant. With its laid-back atmosphere, live music, and stunning views, Eastwest Beach Club is the perfect spot to spend a day by the sea.

6. Sveti Jakov Beach:

- Escape the crowds and discover the tranquility of Sveti Jakov Beach, a hidden gem located just a short walk from Ploče. This secluded beach boasts crystal-clear waters, golden sands, and stunning views of Dubrovnik Old Town and Lokrum Island. Relax on the beach, swim in the azure sea, and soak up the natural beauty of this idyllic coastal paradise.

7. Dubrovnik Sun Gardens Resort:

- Treat yourself to a day of luxury and relaxation at the Dubrovnik Sun Gardens Resort, a five-star resort located in the nearby village of Orasac. Enjoy access to private beaches, swimming pools, and spa facilities, as well as a range of restaurants, bars, and recreational activities. Whether you're looking for a rejuvenating spa treatment or a gourmet dining experience, the Dubrovnik Sun Gardens Resort offers everything you need for a memorable day of indulgence.

8. Water Sports and Activities:

- Get your adrenaline pumping with a variety of water sports and activities available in Ploče. Rent a kayak or stand-up paddleboard and explore the coastline at your own pace, or join a guided snorkeling or scuba diving excursion to discover the underwater world of the Adriatic Sea. From jet skiing and parasailing to sailing and windsurfing, there's no shortage of ways to enjoy the water in Ploče.

PILE:

Pile is the gateway to Dubrovnik's rich history and legendary tales, where every stone has a story to tell. Begin your exploration at the imposing Pile Gate, the main entrance to the Old Town, and marvel at its grandeur and architectural beauty. Step back in time as you wander through the ancient streets, passing historic landmarks like the Lovrijenac

Fortress, the Onofrio's Fountain, and the Sponza Palace. Dive into the world of Game of Thrones with a guided tour of filming locations like the Red Keep and the Walk of Shame, or immerse yourself in the vibrant local culture at the Dubrovnik Summer Festival, where you can enjoy open-air performances of music, theater, and dance against the backdrop of the city's historic landmarks.

What to Do and See

1. Explore Dubrovnik Old Town Walls:

- Start your adventure by exploring the iconic Dubrovnik Old Town walls, which can be accessed from Pile. Walk along the ancient fortifications and enjoy panoramic views of the city, the Adriatic Sea, and the surrounding islands. Don't forget to bring your camera to capture the stunning vistas!

2. Visit Lovrijenac Fortress:

- Marvel at the impressive Lovrijenac Fortress, also known as the "Gibraltar of Dubrovnik." Perched atop a rocky cliff overlooking the sea, this formidable fortress offers breathtaking views and a fascinating glimpse into Dubrovnik's rich history. Explore the fortress's ramparts, towers, and underground chambers, and learn about its role in defending the city from invaders.

3. Walk Down Stradun:

- Take a leisurely stroll down Stradun, the main street of Dubrovnik Old Town, which begins at Pile Gate. Admire the elegant architecture, historic buildings, and charming shops and cafes that line this bustling thoroughfare. Don't miss the chance to snap photos of the iconic landmarks, such as the Church of St. Blaise and the Sponza Palace, along the way.

4. Visit Onofrio's Fountain:

- Stop by Onofrio's Fountain, located just inside Pile Gate, and marvel at this beautiful Renaissance-era fountain. Built in the 15th century to provide the city with fresh water, Onofrio's Fountain features a dome-shaped structure adorned with intricate stone carvings. Take a moment to cool off with a refreshing drink from one of the nearby cafes.

5. Explore Gradac Park:

- Take a break from the hustle and bustle of the city and relax in Gradac Park, a peaceful green oasis located near Pile. Stroll through the park's lush gardens, enjoy panoramic views of the Adriatic Sea, and admire the beautiful sculptures and monuments scattered throughout the park. Gradac Park is the perfect place to unwind and enjoy nature's beauty.

6. Relax at Danče Beach:

- Head down to Danče Beach, a picturesque pebble beach located just a short walk from Pile. Nestled between rocky cliffs and crystal-clear waters, Danče Beach offers a tranquil retreat away from the crowds. Spend the day sunbathing, swimming, and snorkeling in the pristine waters of the Adriatic Sea.

7. Take a Game of Thrones Tour:

- Discover the real-life locations used as filming sites for the hit TV series Game of Thrones with a guided tour departing from Pile. Visit iconic landmarks such as the Red Keep, the Walk of Shame, and the House of the Undying, and learn behind-the-scenes stories and trivia from the show's production.

8. Dine at Local Restaurants:

- Indulge in delicious Croatian cuisine at one of the many restaurants and taverns located in Pile and the surrounding area. Sample fresh seafood dishes, traditional Dalmatian specialties, and locally sourced ingredients prepared with Mediterranean flair. Be sure to try favorites like black risotto, grilled fish, and peka, a slow-cooked meat or seafood dish.

LAPAD:

Lapad is a paradise for nature lovers, beachgoers, and outdoor enthusiasts, offering a perfect blend of natural beauty and modern amenities. Spend your days soaking up the sun on Lapad Beach, where you can swim in the crystal-clear waters, build sandcastles, or enjoy water sports like kayaking and paddleboarding. Explore the scenic Lapad Bay Promenade, lined with palm trees, cafes, and bars, where you can enjoy panoramic views of the Adriatic Sea and the nearby Elaphiti Islands. Don't miss the chance to visit Park Orsula, a hidden gem located on a hilltop overlooking Lapad, where you can enjoy breathtaking views and explore the park's lush gardens and historic landmarks.

What to Do and See

1. Lapad Beach:

- Start your exploration of Lapad with a visit to Lapad Beach, one of the largest and most popular beaches in Dubrovnik. With its crystal-clear waters, sandy shores, and shady pine trees, Lapad Beach is the perfect spot to soak up the sun, swim in the sea, and enjoy water sports like kayaking, paddleboarding, and jet skiing.

2. Sunset Promenade:

- Take a leisurely stroll along Lapad's scenic waterfront promenade, which stretches along the coast from Lapad Beach to Uvala Lapad Bay. Enjoy panoramic views of the Adriatic Sea, Lokrum Island, and the Elaphiti Islands as you walk along the palm-lined promenade, dotted with cafes, restaurants, and shops.

3. Visit Uvala Lapad Bay:

- Explore the tranquil Uvala Lapad Bay, a beautiful natural harbor surrounded by pine-covered hills and rocky cliffs. Relax on the pebble beach, swim in the calm waters, or rent a pedal boat to explore the bay and its hidden coves. With its peaceful ambiance and stunning scenery, Uvala Lapad Bay is the perfect place to escape the hustle and bustle of the city.

4. Park Orsula:

- Discover the hidden gem of Park Orsula, a scenic park located on a hilltop overlooking Lapad and the Adriatic Sea. Take a leisurely stroll through the park's lush gardens, enjoy panoramic views from the viewpoint, and admire the impressive Orsula Church, a beautiful Romanesque-style church dating back to the 13th century.

5. Copacabana Beach:

- Head to Copacabana Beach, a lively beach located in the northern part of Lapad. With its sandy shores, shallow waters, and range of amenities including beach bars, restaurants, and water sports rentals, Copacabana Beach is a favorite spot for locals and tourists alike. Spend the day lounging on a sunbed, playing beach volleyball, or enjoying a refreshing cocktail by the sea.

6. Dubrovnik Copacabana Marina:

- Explore the Dubrovnik Copacabana Marina, a modern marina located adjacent to Copacabana Beach. Admire the sleek yachts and sailboats moored in the marina, and enjoy waterfront dining at one of the marina's restaurants and cafes. Take a leisurely stroll along the waterfront promenade and soak up the vibrant atmosphere of this bustling harbor.

7. Lapad Bay Promenade:

- Walk along the Lapad Bay Promenade, a scenic pathway that runs along the edge of Lapad Bay. Enjoy stunning views of the bay and the surrounding coastline as you stroll past palm trees, gardens, and waterfront cafes. Stop for a drink or a snack at one of the many cafes and bars lining the promenade, and watch the boats sail by as you relax by the sea.

GRUŽ:

Gruž is the gateway to adventure, where you can embark on a journey of discovery and exploration. Explore the bustling Gruž Market, where you can browse stalls overflowing with fresh produce, local delicacies, and handmade crafts, or watch as fishing boats unload their catch of the day at the busy port. Visit the Dubrovnik Copacabana Marina, where you can admire sleek yachts and sailboats, enjoy waterfront dining, or take a leisurely stroll along the waterfront promenade. Don't miss the chance to take a boat trip from Gruž and explore the nearby Elaphiti Islands, where you can swim, snorkel, and sunbathe in secluded coves surrounded by pristine nature.

What to Do and See

1. Gruž Market:

- Start your exploration of Gruž with a visit to the lively Gruž Market, where you can immerse yourself in the sights, sounds, and smells of Dubrovnik's local food scene. Browse stalls piled high with fresh fruits, vegetables, cheeses, olives, and other delicious local produce, and chat with friendly vendors to learn more about Croatian culinary traditions.

2. Port of Gruž:

- Explore the bustling Port of Gruž, one of the largest and busiest ports in Dubrovnik. Watch as fishing boats, yachts, and cruise ships come and go, and soak up the maritime atmosphere of this historic harbor. Take a stroll along the waterfront promenade, lined with cafes, restaurants, and shops, and enjoy panoramic views of the Adriatic Sea and the nearby islands.

3. Visit Lapad Bay:

- Take a short walk from Gruž to Lapad Bay, a beautiful natural harbor located just a stone's throw away. Relax on the sandy beach, swim in the crystal-clear waters, or rent a paddleboard or kayak to explore the bay. Lapad Bay is also home to a range of waterfront restaurants and cafes where you can enjoy fresh seafood dishes and Mediterranean cuisine with a view.

4. Explore Dubrovnik Bridge:

- Marvel at the stunning Dubrovnik Bridge, a modern cable-stayed bridge that spans the Dubrovacka River in Gruž. Take a leisurely walk across the bridge and enjoy panoramic views of the city, the port, and the surrounding area. Don't forget to snap some photos of this impressive architectural feat against the backdrop of the Adriatic Sea.

5. Visit Dubrovnik Main Bus Station:

- Take a stroll to Dubrovnik Main Bus Station, located in Gruž, and marvel at its striking Brutalist architecture. Admire the bold lines, geometric shapes, and concrete facade of this iconic building, which serves as a major transportation hub connecting Dubrovnik with other cities and towns in Croatia and beyond.

6. Dine at Local Restaurants:

- Indulge in delicious Croatian cuisine at one of the many restaurants and taverns located in Gruž. Sample fresh seafood dishes, traditional Dalmatian specialties, and Mediterranean-inspired cuisine, all made with locally sourced ingredients. Be sure to try favorites like black risotto, grilled fish, and peka, a slow-cooked meat or seafood dish.

7. Gruz Open Market:

- Wander through the Gruz Open Market, where you can find a wide range of goods including fresh produce, local delicacies, handmade crafts, and souvenirs. Browse the stalls, chat with local artisans, and pick up unique gifts and mementos to take home with you.

8. Explore the Local Neighborhoods:

- Take some time to explore the charming residential neighborhoods of Gruž, where you can discover hidden gems such as quaint cafes, historic churches, and traditional stone houses. Wander off the beaten path and soak up the authentic local atmosphere as you explore the streets and alleyways of this vibrant neighborhood.

9. Relax at Sunset Beach:

- Head to Sunset Beach, a tranquil cove located near Gruž, and unwind on the pebble shore as you watch the sun dip below the horizon. Enjoy panoramic views of the Adriatic Sea and the nearby islands, and savor the peaceful ambiance of this secluded beach away from the crowds.

10. Take a Boat Trip:

- Embark on a boat trip from Gruž and explore the stunning coastline and islands of the Dubrovnik Riviera. Cruise past rugged cliffs, hidden coves, and pristine beaches, and stop to swim, snorkel, and sunbathe in the crystal-clear waters of the Adriatic Sea. With its scenic beauty and tranquil atmosphere, a boat trip from Gruž is the perfect way to experience the natural wonders of the Dubrovnik region.

BABIN KUK:

Babin Kuk is a paradise for beach lovers, with its pristine shores, crystal-clear waters, and stunning coastal views. Spend your days relaxing on the sandy beaches of Copacabana Beach and Sunset Beach, where you can swim, sunbathe, or enjoy water sports like jet skiing and parasailing. Explore the underwater world of Dubrovnik with a visit to the city's Underwater Museum, located just off the coast of Babin Kuk, where you can discover a unique collection of sculptures and art installations submerged beneath the surface. Don't miss the chance to take a boat trip to Lokrum Island, where you can explore botanical gardens, historic landmarks, and secluded beaches surrounded by lush greenery.

What to Do and See

1. Relax at Copacabana Beach:

- Start your exploration of Babin Kuk with a visit to Copacabana Beach, one of the most popular beaches in Dubrovnik. With its pebble shores, crystal-clear waters, and range of amenities including sunbeds, umbrellas, and beach bars, Copacabana Beach is the perfect spot to relax and soak up the sun.

2. Enjoy Water Sports:

- Get active and enjoy a variety of water sports and activities available at Copacabana Beach.

Rent a kayak or paddleboard and explore the coastline, or join a guided snorkeling or scuba diving excursion to discover the underwater world of the Adriatic Sea. With its calm waters and scenic surroundings, Babin Kuk is the perfect playground for water sports enthusiasts of all levels.

3. Explore Lapad Bay:

- Take a leisurely walk along the scenic waterfront promenade to Lapad Bay, a beautiful natural harbor located nearby. Relax on the sandy beach, swim in the tranquil waters, or rent a pedal boat to explore the bay and its hidden coves. Lapad Bay is also home to a range of waterfront restaurants and cafes where you can enjoy fresh seafood dishes and Mediterranean cuisine with a view.

4. Visit Dubrovnik's Underwater Museum:

- Dive into the depths of the Adriatic Sea and explore Dubrovnik's Underwater Museum, located just off the coast of Babin Kuk. Discover a unique collection of sculptures and art installations submerged beneath the surface, creating an immersive underwater gallery that's unlike anything you've ever seen before.

5. Take a Boat Trip to Lokrum Island:

- Embark on a boat trip from Babin Kuk to Lokrum Island, a beautiful nature reserve located just a short ferry ride away. Explore the island's lush botanical gardens, historic landmarks, and secluded beaches, and keep an eye out for peacocks roaming freely throughout the park. Don't miss the chance to hike to the top of Fort Royal for panoramic views of Dubrovnik and the surrounding area.

6. Explore Cave Bar More:

- Venture into the heart of Babin Kuk and discover Cave Bar More, a unique underground bar located beneath the Hotel More. Descend into the natural cave formations and enjoy drinks in a one-of-a-kind setting surrounded by stalactites, stalagmites, and shimmering rock pools. With its intimate ambiance and stunning surroundings, Cave Bar More offers a memorable drinking experience unlike any other.

7. Discover the Elaphiti Islands:

- Set sail from Babin Kuk and explore the nearby Elaphiti Islands, a stunning archipelago consisting of 13 islands scattered along the Dubrovnik Riviera. Cruise past rugged cliffs, hidden coves, and pristine beaches, and stop to swim, snorkel, and sunbathe in the crystal-clear waters of the

Adriatic Sea. With their natural beauty and unspoiled landscapes, the Elaphiti Islands are a paradise waiting to be discovered.

MOKOŠICA:

Mokošica is a hidden gem nestled along the banks of the scenic Rijeka Dubrovačka river, offering a peaceful retreat away from the hustle and bustle of the city. Explore the historic Church of St. Jerome, a beautiful Baroque-style church dating back to the 16th century, or cross the picturesque Old Stone Bridge and admire panoramic views of the river and surrounding countryside. Relax and unwind along the riverfront promenade, where you can enjoy scenic views, charming cafes, and tranquil parks and gardens. Don't miss the chance to explore nearby nature trails, where you can hike through lush forests, discover hidden waterfalls, and enjoy picnics in the great outdoors.

What to Do and See

1. Explore the Riverfront Promenade:

- Start your exploration of Mokošica with a leisurely stroll along the riverfront promenade. Enjoy picturesque views of the river, dotted with boats and lined with quaint cafes and restaurants. Take in the tranquil ambiance as you walk beneath the shade of palm trees and admire the traditional stone houses that line the waterfront.

2. Visit the Church of St. Jerome:

- Discover the historic Church of St. Jerome, a beautiful Baroque-style church located in the heart of Mokošica. Admire the intricate architecture, ornate decorations, and stunning artwork inside the church, and learn about its fascinating history dating back to the 16th century. Don't miss the chance to attend a traditional church service or concert to experience the local culture firsthand.

3. Explore the Old Stone Bridge:

- Cross the picturesque Old Stone Bridge, a historic landmark that spans the Rijeka Dubrovačka river and connects Mokošica with neighboring areas. Marvel at the ancient stone arches, intricate carvings, and panoramic views of the surrounding countryside as you walk across the bridge. Don't forget to snap some photos of this iconic structure against the backdrop of the river and lush greenery.

4. Relax at ACI Marina Dubrovnik:

- Head to ACI Marina Dubrovnik, located near Mokošica, and relax in the scenic surroundings of this modern marina. Admire the sleek yachts and sailboats moored in the marina, and enjoy waterfront dining at one of the marina's restaurants and cafes. Take a leisurely stroll along the waterfront promenade and soak up the vibrant atmosphere of this bustling harbor.

5. Take a Boat Tour:

- Embark on a boat tour from Mokošica and explore the stunning coastline and islands of the Dubrovnik Riviera. Cruise along the Rijeka Dubrovačka river, past lush green hillsides, hidden coves, and charming seaside villages. Stop to swim, snorkel, and sunbathe in the crystal-clear waters of the Adriatic Sea, and enjoy panoramic views of the surrounding landscape from the deck of your boat.

6. Visit the Franciscan Monastery in Rožat:

- Take a short drive from Mokošica to the nearby village of Rožat and visit the Franciscan Monastery, a historic landmark dating back to the 15th century. Explore the monastery's beautiful courtyard, gardens, and chapel, and learn about the life of the Franciscan monks who have lived here for centuries. Don't miss the chance to see the monastery's impressive collection of religious artifacts and artworks.

7. Explore Nearby Nature Trails:

- Lace up your hiking boots and explore the nearby nature trails that wind through the hillsides surrounding Mokošica. Enjoy scenic views of the river, forests, and countryside as you hike along well-marked trails that lead to hidden waterfalls, viewpoints, and picnic spots. Keep an eye out for native wildlife such as birds, butterflies, and lizards as you explore the natural beauty of this picturesque region.

GETTING THERE AND MOVING DUBROVNIK

Fellow explorer, let's talk about getting to Dubrovnik and moving around this stunning city in style! Buckle up, because we're about to embark on an adventure that's as thrilling as a ride on a Croatian rollercoaster.

First things first: how do you actually get to Dubrovnik? Well, if you're feeling fancy, you can hop on a plane and jet-set your way to Dubrovnik Airport, conveniently located just outside the city. From there, you can catch a scenic bus ride or hop in a taxi to whisk you away to the heart of Dubrovnik's Old Town. Just imagine the excitement as you soar through the skies, eagerly anticipating the breathtaking views that await you on the ground below.

But maybe you're more of a road trip aficionado – in which case, pack your bags, rev up your engine, and hit the open road! Dubrovnik is easily accessible by car, with well-maintained highways leading straight to its historic center. Just be sure to take plenty of pit stops along the way to soak in the stunning scenery and snap some envy-inducing Instagram photos.

Now that you've arrived in Dubrovnik, it's time to explore! And what better way to do that than by hopping on one of the city's iconic buses?

45

Dubrovnik's public transportation system is a breeze to navigate, with frequent buses whisking you away to all the must-see sights and attractions. From the historic charm of the Old Town to the sun-soaked shores of Banje Beach, there's no shortage of adventures waiting to be had.

As for popular stops, you won't want to miss the Pile Gate, the main entrance to Dubrovnik's Old Town and a hub of activity and excitement. From there, you can stroll along the ancient city walls, explore the maze-like streets, and soak up the atmosphere of this historic gem.

And when it's time to catch your breath and refuel, head over to the bustling Gruž Harbor, where you'll find a vibrant market overflowing with fresh produce, local delicacies, and plenty of opportunities for people-watching. Trust me, you'll want to sample everything in sight!

WHERE TO EAT IN DUBROVNIK

Ah, prepare your taste buds for a culinary journey through the flavors of Dubrovnik! From fresh seafood to mouthwatering Mediterranean dishes, this city is a foodie's paradise just waiting to be explored. So grab your fork and let's dive into some of the top restaurants in Dubrovnik, where every bite is a delicious adventure.

Nautika Restaurant:

- Location: Located right on the edge of the sea, Nautika offers stunning views of the Adriatic Sea and the historic walls of Dubrovnik.

- Menu Highlights: Start your meal with a plate of freshly shucked oysters, followed by a mouthwatering seafood risotto bursting with flavor. For the main course, indulge in the catch of the day, grilled to perfection and served with seasonal vegetables. And don't forget to save room for dessert – the chocolate fondant with vanilla ice cream is a must-try!

Proto Restaurant:

- Location: Tucked away in Dubrovnik's charming Old Town, Proto exudes old-world charm and elegance.

- Menu Highlights: Begin your culinary journey with a selection of Dalmatian prosciutto and local cheeses, served with homemade bread and olives. For the main course, savor the lobster pasta, tossed in a rich tomato sauce with hints of garlic and fresh herbs. And be sure to leave room for Proto's signature dessert – the indulgent chocolate soufflé, served warm and oozing with decadence.

360° Dubrovnik:

- Location: Perched atop the city walls, 360° Dubrovnik offers panoramic views of the Old Town and the shimmering sea.

- Menu Highlights: Start your meal with a refreshing salad of local greens, tomatoes, and olives, drizzled with a tangy citrus vinaigrette. For the main course, feast on the grilled Adriatic sea bass, served with roasted potatoes and sautéed vegetables. And don't miss the opportunity to sample one of 360° Dubrovnik's signature cocktails, like the refreshing Lavender Mojito or the zesty Citrus Spritz.

Restaurant Dubrovnik:

- Location: Located in the heart of the Old Town, Restaurant Dubrovnik invites diners to enjoy traditional Croatian cuisine in a charming courtyard setting.

- Menu Highlights: Start your meal with a plate of freshly grilled calamari, served with garlic-infused olive oil and a squeeze of lemon. For the main course, indulge in the slow-cooked lamb shank, tender and flavorful, served with creamy mashed potatoes and seasonal vegetables. And be sure to save room for dessert – the homemade apple strudel, served warm with a dollop of vanilla ice cream, is a true delight!

- **Bota Šare Restaurant:**

- Location: Nestled in the heart of Dubrovnik's Old Town, Bota Šare offers a cozy and inviting atmosphere with a touch of rustic charm.

- Menu Highlights: Start your gastronomic journey with a platter of freshly shucked Adriatic oysters, served with a squeeze of lemon and a dash of homemade mignonette sauce. For the main course, indulge in the grilled octopus, tender and flavorful, served with creamy mashed potatoes and grilled vegetables. And don't miss out on their selection of local wines to complement your meal – the Dingač red wine pairs perfectly with seafood dishes.

- **Pantarul Restaurant**:

- Location: Located just outside the city walls, Pantarul offers a relaxed and welcoming atmosphere with a focus on fresh, locally-sourced ingredients.

- Menu Highlights: Start your culinary adventure with the homemade goat cheese bruschetta, topped with caramelized onions and drizzled with balsamic glaze. For the main course, savor the slow-cooked pork shoulder, tender and succulent, served with roasted potatoes and seasonal vegetables. And be sure to leave room for dessert – the decadent chocolate lava cake, served with a scoop of homemade vanilla ice cream, is a true indulgence.

- **Azur Restaurant**:

- Location: Situated just steps away from the historic walls of Dubrovnik, Azur offers a unique fusion of Mediterranean and Asian flavors in a chic and stylish setting.

- Menu Highlights: Start your culinary journey with the crispy duck spring rolls, served with a tangy hoisin dipping sauce. For the main course, indulge in the seafood curry, bursting with fresh shrimp, mussels, and calamari in a fragrant coconut broth. And don't miss out on their selection of craft cocktails – the Lychee Martini is a refreshing choice to accompany your meal.

- **Taj Mahal Dubrovnik**:

- Location: Located in the heart of the Old Town, Taj Mahal Dubrovnik brings a taste of the exotic to Dubrovnik with its authentic Bosnian cuisine and warm, inviting atmosphere.

- Menu Highlights: Start your culinary journey with the traditional Bosnian mezze platter, featuring a selection of savory dips, spreads, and grilled meats. For the main course, indulge in the lamb kebabs, tender and flavorful, served with fluffy rice and grilled vegetables. And be sure to save room for dessert – the baklava, sweet and flaky, is the perfect way to end your meal on a high note.

Direction

1. **Nautika Restaurant**:

- Location: Located near Pile Gate, the main entrance to Dubrovnik's Old Town, at Brsalje 3.

- Directions: From Pile Gate, head towards the city walls and follow the path along the water. Nautika Restaurant will be on your left, just before you reach the entrance to Fort Lovrijenac.

2. **Proto Restaurant**:

    - Location: Situated in the heart of Dubrovnik's Old Town, on Siroka ulica 1.

    - Directions: From Stradun, the main street in the Old Town, turn onto Siroka ulica and continue straight. Proto Restaurant will be on your left, just a short walk from the main square.

3. **360° Dubrovnik**:

    - Location: Located atop the city walls near Ploce Gate, at Ul. kralja Petra Krešimira IV 1.

    - Directions: From Ploce Gate, follow the path along the city walls towards the entrance to Fort Revelin. 360° Dubrovnik will be on your left, offering stunning views of the Old Town and the Adriatic Sea.

4. **Restaurant Dubrovnik:**

    - Location: Found within Dubrovnik's Old Town, at Prijeko ul. 24.

    - Directions: From Stradun, head towards the Cathedral and turn onto Prijeko ulica. Continue straight and Restaurant Dubrovnik will be on your right, nestled in a charming courtyard.

5. **Bota Šare Restaurant:**

    - Location: Located in Dubrovnik's Old Town, at Od Sigurate 1.

    - Directions: From Stradun, head towards the Cathedral and turn onto Od Sigurate. Bota Šare Restaurant will be on your left, just a short walk from the main square.

6. **Pantarul Restaurant:**

    - Location: Situated just outside the city walls, at Nikole Gučetića 2.

    - Directions: From Ploce Gate, head towards the Cable Car station and continue straight. Pantarul Restaurant will be on your right, offering a cozy retreat from the hustle and bustle of the Old Town.

7. **Azur Restaurant:**

- Location: Found near the Ploce Gate, at Pobijana ul. 10.

- Directions: From Ploce Gate, head towards the Cable Car station and turn onto Pobijana ulica. Azur Restaurant will be on your left, offering a unique fusion of Mediterranean and Asian flavors.

8. **Taj Mahal Dubrovnik**:

    - Location: Located in Dubrovnik's Old Town, at Nikole Gučetića 2.

    - Directions: From Stradun, head towards the Cathedral and turn onto Nikole Gučetića. Taj Mahal Dubrovnik will be on your right, serving up authentic Bosnian cuisine in a warm and inviting atmosphere.

TOP CUISINE TO TRY OUT IN DUBROVNIK

Get ready to embark on a culinary adventure through the flavors of Dubrovnik! From fresh seafood to hearty traditional dishes, Dubrovnik's cuisine is a mouthwatering fusion of Mediterranean and Balkan influences. So put on your stretchy pants and let's dive into the top cuisine you absolutely must try in Dubrovnik:

1. **Seafood Delights**: With its stunning coastline along the Adriatic Sea, it's no surprise that seafood reigns supreme in Dubrovnik. Start your culinary journey with a plate of freshly shucked oysters, briny and succulent, or dive into a bowl of creamy seafood risotto, bursting with the flavors of the sea. Don't miss the chance to sample local specialties like grilled octopus, calamari, and black risotto made with cuttlefish ink – each bite is a taste of the ocean!

2. **Dalmatian Prosciutto and Cheese**: Indulge in the flavors of the Dalmatian coast with a platter of thinly sliced prosciutto, cured to perfection and bursting with savory goodness. Pair it with a selection of local cheeses, like Pag cheese or sheep's milk cheese, for a truly unforgettable culinary experience. Add some olives, homemade

bread, and a glass of local wine, and you've got yourself the perfect Mediterranean feast!

3. **Peka**: Prepare your taste buds for a hearty and delicious traditional dish known as peka. This slow-cooked masterpiece features tender meats like lamb, veal, or octopus, combined with potatoes, onions, and herbs, all cooked to perfection under a bell-shaped lid. The result? A melt-in-your-mouth sensation that's packed with flavor and guaranteed to leave you coming back for more.

4. **Brodetto**: Get ready to slurp up every last drop of this flavorful fish stew, known as brodetto. Made with a variety of locally caught fish, shellfish, tomatoes, and aromatic herbs, brodetto is a hearty and comforting dish that's perfect for warming up on a chilly evening. Be sure to mop up the rich broth with a slice of crusty bread – trust me, it's the best part!

5. **Rozata**: No meal in Dubrovnik is complete without indulging in a sweet treat known as rozata. This creamy custard pudding, similar to crème caramel, is flavored with rose water or citrus zest and topped with a caramelized sugar glaze. It's the perfect way to end your meal on a sweet note and satisfy your sweet tooth in true Dubrovnik style.

6. **Black Risotto (Crni Rižot)**: Don't let the dark color scare you – black risotto is a

culinary gem of Dubrovnik that you simply must try. Made with squid or cuttlefish ink, this rich and flavorful dish is cooked with Arborio rice, onions, garlic, white wine, and a touch of olive oil. The result is a creamy, savory risotto with a subtle hint of the sea. Pair it with a glass of crisp white wine and prepare to be transported to culinary heaven.

7. **Ston Oysters**: Just a short drive from Dubrovnik lies the town of Ston, known for its pristine waters and delicious oysters. These briny bivalves are prized for their plump texture and delicate flavor, making them a must-try delicacy for seafood lovers. Whether you enjoy them freshly shucked on the half shell or grilled with a squeeze of lemon, Ston oysters are sure to tantalize your taste buds and leave you craving more.

8. **Pag Cheese**: Made from the milk of sheep that graze on the rocky pastures of the island of Pag, Pag cheese is a true taste of the Adriatic. This hard, aged cheese is known for its distinct flavor, which is both salty and savory with a hint of sweetness. Enjoy it sliced thinly on a cheese platter or paired with local honey for a deliciously indulgent treat that perfectly captures the flavors of the region.

9. **Fritule**: For a sweet snack that's perfect for satisfying your sweet tooth on the go, look no

further than fritule. These small, fried dough balls are flavored with rum, lemon zest, and sometimes raisins, then dusted with powdered sugar for an extra touch of sweetness. Whether enjoyed as a midday snack or a post-dinner treat, fritule are a beloved tradition in Dubrovnik and a delicious way to experience the city's culinary heritage.

10. **Rakija**: No culinary journey through Dubrovnik would be complete without sampling a glass of rakija, the traditional fruit brandy beloved throughout Croatia. Made from a variety of fruits, including grapes, plums, and cherries, rakija is often enjoyed as a digestif after a hearty meal. Sip it slowly and savor the complex flavors, or use it as a base for cocktails – either way, rakija is sure to add a touch of Croatian flair to your dining experience in Dubrovnik.

TOP ATTRACTIONS

Get ready to embark on an adventure through the enchanting city of Dubrovnik! From ancient city walls to sun-soaked beaches, Dubrovnik is a treasure trove of unforgettable experiences just waiting to be discovered. So pack your bags, grab your camera, and let's dive into the top attractions that will make your visit to Dubrovnik one for the ages:

1. **Dubrovnik City Walls**: Step back in time as you stroll along the iconic Dubrovnik City Walls, which encircle the historic Old Town like a protective embrace. Take in breathtaking panoramic views of terracotta rooftops, shimmering sea, and rugged cliffs as you follow the path along the walls – just be sure to bring plenty of water and sunscreen, as the sun can be fierce!

2. **Old Town**: Lose yourself in the maze-like streets of Dubrovnik's Old Town, where history comes alive around every corner. Marvel at ancient churches, historic palaces, and charming squares as you wander through narrow alleys lined with centuries-old buildings. Don't miss must-see sights like Stradun, the main street of the Old Town, and the ornate Rector's Palace, which offers a glimpse into Dubrovnik's rich history.

3. **Fort Lovrijenac**: Perched dramatically atop a rocky outcrop overlooking the sea, Fort Lovrijenac is a formidable fortress that has stood guard over Dubrovnik for centuries. Explore its imposing walls and take in sweeping views of the Adriatic Sea and the Old Town below – just be prepared to climb a few stairs to reach the top!

4. **Banje Beach**: When it's time to relax and soak up the sun, head to Banje Beach, Dubrovnik's most famous stretch of sand. Lounge on a sunbed and feel the warm Mediterranean sun on your skin, or take a refreshing dip in the crystal-clear waters of the Adriatic Sea. With its vibrant beach club scene and stunning views of the Old Town, Banje Beach is the perfect place to unwind and enjoy a taste of paradise.

5. **Mount Srđ**: For panoramic views that will take your breath away, hop on the Dubrovnik Cable Car and ascend to the summit of Mount Srđ. From the observation deck at the top, you'll be treated to 360-degree views of Dubrovnik, the Adriatic Sea, and the surrounding islands – a perfect spot for capturing unforgettable photos and making memories that will last a lifetime.

6. **Lokrum Island**: Escape the hustle and bustle of the city and embark on a day trip to Lokrum

Island, just a short ferry ride from Dubrovnik's Old Port. Explore lush botanical gardens, wander through ancient ruins, and relax on secluded beaches surrounded by crystal-clear waters. Keep an eye out for peacocks roaming freely around the island – they're a colorful and charming sight to behold!

7. **Dubrovnik Cathedral**: Step inside the ornate Dubrovnik Cathedral, also known as the Cathedral of the Assumption of the Virgin Mary, and marvel at its stunning Baroque architecture and richly decorated interior. Admire intricate stone carvings, gilded altars, and beautiful stained glass windows as you explore this sacred space – just be sure to dress respectfully and observe any posted guidelines.

8. **Game of Thrones Tours**: Calling all fans of the hit TV series Game of Thrones – Dubrovnik is your real-life King's Landing! Embark on a guided tour of filming locations used in the show, including the iconic Red Keep, the streets of Flea Bottom, and the steps of the Great Sept of Baelor. Whether you're a die-hard fan or just curious to see where the magic happened, a Game of Thrones tour is a must-do experience in Dubrovnik.

9. **Dubrovnik Aquarium and Maritime Museum**: Dive into Dubrovnik's maritime history at the Dubrovnik Aquarium and

Maritime Museum, located in the historic fortress of St. John's Fortress. Explore fascinating exhibits showcasing marine life from the Adriatic Sea, as well as artifacts and interactive displays detailing Dubrovnik's rich maritime heritage. It's a fun and educational experience for visitors of all ages!

10. **Dubrovnik Cable Car**: For an exhilarating ride and stunning panoramic views, hop aboard the Dubrovnik Cable Car. Ascend to the summit of Mount Srđ in just a few minutes, where you'll be treated to breathtaking vistas of the Old Town, Lokrum Island, and the shimmering Adriatic Sea stretching out before you. Don't forget to bring your camera – the views from the top are picture-perfect!

11. **Dubrovnik City Harbor**: Take a leisurely stroll along Dubrovnik's picturesque harbor and soak in the sights and sounds of this bustling maritime hub. Watch as fishing boats bob gently in the water, yachts glide gracefully into port, and seagulls swoop and dive overhead. For a truly memorable experience, hop on a boat tour and explore the nearby Elaphiti Islands or the scenic coastline of the Dubrovnik Riviera.

12. **War Photo Limited**: Gain insight into Dubrovnik's recent history at War Photo Limited, a thought-provoking museum

dedicated to photojournalism and the impact of war on society. Browse powerful exhibits showcasing images from conflicts around the world, as well as exhibitions focusing on the Croatian War of Independence and its effects on Dubrovnik. It's a sobering yet important reminder of the resilience of the human spirit in the face of adversity.

13. **Dubrovnik Summer Festival**: If you're visiting Dubrovnik in the summer months, don't miss the chance to experience the Dubrovnik Summer Festival – a celebration of music, theater, dance, and cultural heritage. From open-air concerts in historic squares to theatrical performances in ancient fortresses, the festival brings the city to life with a vibrant array of artistic performances and events. Join the festivities and immerse yourself in Dubrovnik's rich cultural heritage.

14. **Buža Bar**: For a truly unforgettable experience, seek out Buža Bar – a hidden gem tucked away on the cliffs just outside Dubrovnik's city walls. Follow the signs marked "Cold Drinks" or "Buža" and descend down a narrow staircase carved into the rock until you reach this magical seaside bar. Grab a seat on the terrace overlooking the Adriatic Sea, sip on a refreshing cocktail, and watch the sun sink below the horizon in a blaze of color – it's a moment you'll never forget.

15. **Sponza Palace**: Step back in time as you explore the elegant Sponza Palace, a Renaissance-era building located in Dubrovnik's Old Town. Admire its striking Venetian Gothic architecture, intricate stone carvings, and stunning courtyard as you learn about its fascinating history as a customs house, mint, and treasury. Be sure to check out the Memorial Room, which pays tribute to the defenders of Dubrovnik during the Croatian War of Independence.

TOP ACCOMMODATION

Ahoy, fellow traveler! Get ready to kick back and relax in style as we explore the top accommodations in Dubrovnik. From luxurious hotels to charming guesthouses, Dubrovnik offers a range of options to suit every taste and budget. So let's dive in and discover where you'll be laying your head in this Croatian gem:

Hotel Excelsior Dubrovnik:

- Nestled on the shores of the Adriatic Sea, Hotel Excelsior Dubrovnik exudes elegance and sophistication at every turn. With stunning views of the Old Town and luxurious amenities like a spa, infinity pool, and gourmet restaurants, this iconic hotel is the epitome of luxury. Imagine sipping cocktails on the terrace as the sun sets over the shimmering sea – pure bliss!

Villa Dubrovnik:

- Perched on a cliff overlooking the sea, Villa Dubrovnik offers a secluded retreat just steps away from the bustling Old Town. With its sleek, modern design, private beach, and panoramic views of Lokrum Island, this exclusive boutique hotel is the perfect place to unwind and escape the hustle and bustle of everyday life. Indulge in a massage at the spa, take a dip in the infinity pool, or simply soak up the sun on the terrace – the choice is yours!

Pucic Palace:

- Step back in time as you enter the historic Pucic Palace, a beautifully restored 18th-century building located in the heart of Dubrovnik's Old Town. With its elegant rooms, marble bathrooms, and charming courtyard, this boutique hotel offers a luxurious yet intimate atmosphere that's perfect for romantic getaways or special occasions. Plus, with its prime location just steps away from Stradun, you'll have easy access to all the sights and attractions Dubrovnik has to offer.

Hotel Bellevue Dubrovnik:

- Tucked away on a cliffside overlooking Miramare Bay, Hotel Bellevue Dubrovnik offers a tranquil retreat away from the hustle and bustle of the city center. With its minimalist design, spacious rooms, and breathtaking views of the Adriatic Sea, this boutique hotel is the perfect place to unwind and recharge. Relax by the indoor pool, indulge in a spa treatment, or savor a gourmet meal at the hotel's award-winning restaurant – the choice is yours!

Guesthouse Victoria:

- For a charming and budget-friendly option in the heart of the Old Town, look no further than Guesthouse Victoria. Located just steps away from Stradun, this cozy guesthouse offers comfortable rooms, friendly hospitality, and a warm, inviting atmosphere that will make you feel right at home. Plus, with its convenient location, you'll have easy access to all the sights, shops, and restaurants Dubrovnik has to offer – talk about a win-win!

Villa Glavić:

- Situated just a short walk from the Old Town, Villa Glavić offers a peaceful oasis surrounded by lush gardens and stunning sea views. With its comfortable rooms, outdoor pool, and sun terrace, this charming hotel is the perfect place to relax and recharge after a day of exploring Dubrovnik. Plus, with its friendly staff and warm hospitality, you'll feel right at home from the moment you arrive – talk about a slice of paradise!

- **Hotel Lapad**:
- Nestled in the Lapad Bay area, Hotel Lapad offers a blend of modern comforts and traditional charm. With its spacious rooms, outdoor pool, and panoramic views of the Adriatic Sea, this family-friendly hotel is the perfect base for exploring Dubrovnik and its surrounding areas. Plus, with its convenient location just a short walk from the beach and a quick bus ride to the Old Town, you'll have easy access to all the sights and attractions Dubrovnik has to offer.
- **Hotel Kompas Dubrovnik**:
- Situated on the Lapad Peninsula, Hotel Kompas Dubrovnik boasts stunning sea views, sleek contemporary design, and world-class amenities. Whether you're lounging by the infinity pool, indulging in a spa treatment, or savoring a gourmet meal at the hotel's rooftop restaurant, you'll be treated to unparalleled luxury and comfort at every turn. Plus, with its prime location just steps away from the beach and a short bus ride to the Old Town, you'll have everything you need for a memorable stay in Dubrovnik.

- **Hostel Angelina Old Town:**
- For budget-conscious travelers looking to stay in the heart of the action, Hostel Angelina Old Town is the perfect choice. Located within the walls of Dubrovnik's Old Town, this cozy hostel offers dormitory-style rooms and private accommodations at affordable prices. With its friendly staff, communal kitchen, and lively atmosphere, Hostel Angelina Old Town is the ideal base for exploring Dubrovnik's historic sights, vibrant nightlife, and bustling streets.
- **Rixos Premium Dubrovnik:**
- Experience the height of luxury at Rixos Premium Dubrovnik, a five-star hotel nestled on the shores of the Adriatic Sea. With its elegant rooms, private beach, and world-class amenities, this upscale resort offers an unparalleled level of comfort and sophistication. Whether you're unwinding in the spa, dining at one of the hotel's gourmet restaurants, or soaking up the sun by the infinity pool, you'll be treated to a truly unforgettable experience at Rixos Premium Dubrovnik.
- **Hotel More Dubrovnik:**

- Perched on a cliffside overlooking the Adriatic Sea, Hotel More Dubrovnik offers a unique blend of natural beauty and contemporary luxury. With its sleek design, spacious rooms, and stunning sea views, this boutique hotel is the perfect retreat for travelers seeking tranquility and relaxation. Whether you're enjoying a cocktail at the hotel's Cave Bar, lounging on the private beach, or exploring the nearby Elaphiti Islands, you'll be surrounded by beauty and elegance at every turn.

- **Villa Dubrovnik**:
- Escape to paradise at Villa Dubrovnik, a luxurious retreat located just steps away from Dubrovnik's Old Town. With its sleek design, infinity pool, and panoramic views of the Adriatic Sea, this exclusive villa offers a private oasis for discerning travelers. Whether you're enjoying a gourmet meal prepared by a private chef, relaxing in the sauna, or soaking up the sun on the terrace, you'll be treated to unparalleled luxury and elegance at Villa Dubrovnik.

- **Villa Orsula Dubrovnik**:
- Experience the charm of Dubrovnik's Old Town at Villa Orsula Dubrovnik, a

boutique hotel nestled amidst lush gardens and stunning sea views. With its elegant rooms, outdoor pool, and personalized service, this intimate hotel offers a peaceful retreat away from the hustle and bustle of the city. Whether you're sipping champagne on the terrace, exploring the nearby beaches, or strolling through the historic streets, you'll be surrounded by beauty and tranquility at Villa Orsula Dubrovnik.

Direction

Hotel Excelsior Dubrovnik:

- Location: Frana Supila 12, 20000, Dubrovnik, Croatia.

Villa Dubrovnik:

- Location: Vlaha Bukovca 6, 20000, Dubrovnik, Croatia..

Pucic Palace:

- Location: Ulica od Puča 1, 20000, Dubrovnik, Croatia.

Hotel Bellevue Dubrovnik:

- Location: Pera Čingrije 7, 20000, Dubrovnik, Croatia.

Guesthouse Victoria:

- Location: Prijeko 12, 20000, Dubrovnik, Croatia.

Villa Glavić:

- Location: Pera Čingrije 7, 20000, Dubrovnik, Croatia.

- **Hotel Lapad**:

- Location: Lapadska obala 37, 20000, Dubrovnik, Croatia.

- **Hotel Kompas Dubrovnik**:

- Location: Kardinala Stepinca 21, 20000, Dubrovnik, Croatia.

- **Hostel Angelina Old Town**:

- Location: Zvijezdićeva 1, 20000, Dubrovnik, Croatia.

- **Rixos Premium Dubrovnik**:

- Location: Liechtensteinov put 3, 20000, Dubrovnik, Croatia.

- **Hotel More Dubrovnik**:

- Location: Kardinala Stepinca 33, 20000, Dubrovnik, Croatia.

- **Villa Dubrovnik**:

- Location: Vlaha Bukovca 6, 20000, Dubrovnik, Croatia.

- Directions: Villa Dubrovnik is located
Villa Orsula Dubrovnik:

- Location: Frana Supila 14, 20000, Dubrovnik, Croatia.

SHOPPING AND SOUVENIRS IN DUBROVNIK

Ahoy, fellow treasure seekers! Welcome to the shopper's paradise of Dubrovnik, where the streets are lined with treasures waiting to be discovered and the air is filled with the scent of adventure. From bustling markets to charming boutiques, Dubrovnik offers a wealth of shopping destinations that are sure to satisfy even the most discerning shopper. So, grab your map and let's embark on a whimsical shopping journey through the enchanting streets of Dubrovnik:

1. **Stradun Splendor**:
   - Picture yourself strolling down the cobblestone streets of Dubrovnik's main thoroughfare, Stradun, surrounded by ancient architecture and vibrant energy. This bustling promenade is lined with an eclectic mix of shops and boutiques, offering everything from designer fashion to handmade crafts. So, channel your inner fashionista, browse through the latest trends, and treat yourself to a stylish souvenir that will make you the envy of all your friends back home.

2. **Old Town Markets Marvel**:

- Dive into the vibrant chaos of Dubrovnik's Old Town markets, where the sights, sounds, and smells will transport you to a world of culinary delights and cultural wonders. From the colorful stalls of the Gundulićeva Poljana Market to the bustling Market at Gruž Harbor, these markets are a feast for the senses. So, sharpen your bargaining skills, sample the local delicacies, and pick up some fresh produce or handmade crafts to take home with you.

3. **Artisan Alleyways**:
    - Wander off the beaten path and explore Dubrovnik's charming alleyways, where hidden gems and local treasures await. From quaint artisan shops tucked away in centuries-old buildings to quirky galleries showcasing the work of local artists, these alleyways are a haven for art lovers and collectors alike. So, unleash your inner curator, discover a masterpiece in the making, and bring home a piece of Dubrovnik's vibrant arts scene.

4. **Seaside Souvenirs**:
    - Head down to Dubrovnik's picturesque waterfront and discover a treasure trove

of seaside souvenirs. From nautical-themed trinkets to handmade seashell jewelry, these waterfront shops are the perfect place to find a memento of your seaside adventures. So, grab a gelato, take a leisurely stroll along the promenade, and browse through the seaside stalls as you soak in the stunning views of the Adriatic Sea.

5. **Game of Thrones Goodies**:
   - Calling all Game of Thrones fans – Dubrovnik is your real-life King's Landing! Dive into the world of Westeros and explore the city's Game of Thrones-themed shops, where you'll find everything from replica swords and armor to House sigil banners and dragon figurines. So, don your House colors, pledge your allegiance to your favorite house, and bring home a piece of the Seven Kingdoms to adorn your castle walls.

6. **Lavender Lane**:
   - Immerse yourself in the fragrant world of lavender and discover the soothing scent of Dubrovnik's lavender shops. From fragrant sachets and essential oils to lavender-infused chocolates and liquors, these shops offer a myriad of

lavender-infused delights that are sure to delight your senses. So, take a deep breath, inhale the calming aroma, and let the soothing scent of lavender transport you to a state of relaxation and bliss.

7. **Local Libations**:

- Raise a glass to your Dubrovnik adventure with a visit to one of the city's local liquor shops, where you'll find a tantalizing array of Croatian wines, spirits, and liqueurs. From crisp white wines to robust reds and traditional fruit brandies, these local libations are the perfect way to toast to your travels and bring home a taste of Croatia's rich culinary heritage. So, pick up a bottle of your favorite tipple, share a toast with newfound friends, and savor the flavors of Dubrovnik long after your journey has ended.

VIBRANT NIGHTLIFE OF ARGENTINA

Party people! Prepare to paint the town red in the vibrant nightlife scene of Dubrovnik, where the music is pumping, the drinks are flowing, and the good times never end. From lively bars to pulsating clubs, Dubrovnik offers a nightlife experience that's sure to keep you dancing 'til dawn. So, slip into your dancing shoes and let's dive into the top clubs and hotspots that are lighting up the nights in Dubrovnik:

Revelry on the Rocks at Cave Bar More:

- Picture this: you're sipping cocktails in a cave carved into a cliffside, surrounded by ancient stone walls and breathtaking sea views. Welcome to Cave Bar More, one of Dubrovnik's most unique nightlife venues. With its intimate atmosphere, stunning setting, and eclectic mix of music, this cave bar is the perfect place to kick off your night in style. So, grab a drink, soak in the ambiance, and get ready to dance the night away in this one-of-a-kind hotspot.

Beachfront Bliss at Copacabana Beach Club:

- Who says the party has to stop when the sun goes down? Head to Copacabana Beach Club and keep the beach vibes going all night long. Located just a short drive from Dubrovnik's city center, this beachfront club offers a lively atmosphere, live music, and DJs spinning the hottest tracks until the early hours of the morning. So, kick off your shoes, feel the sand between your toes, and get ready to dance under the stars at this beachside paradise.

Electrifying Energy at Culture Club Revelin:

- Get ready to experience the ultimate party atmosphere at Culture Club Revelin, Dubrovnik's premier nightlife destination. Housed in a historic fortress overlooking the city's ancient walls, this club is a magnet for partygoers from near and far. With its state-of-the-art sound system, dazzling light shows, and world-class DJs, Culture Club Revelin is the place to see and be seen in Dubrovnik. So, don your most stylish threads, prepare to dance 'til dawn, and let the music move you at this electrifying hotspot.

Rooftop Rendezvous at Sky Bar:

- Elevate your nightlife experience to new heights at Sky Bar, Dubrovnik's chic rooftop lounge. Perched atop the iconic Dubrovnik Hotel, this rooftop oasis offers panoramic views of the city skyline and the sparkling Adriatic Sea. Sip on handcrafted cocktails, groove to the beats of resident DJs, and mingle with fellow revelers as you take in the breathtaking vistas from this sky-high hotspot. So, raise a glass to the good life and make memories that will last a lifetime at Sky Bar.

Reggae Rhythms at Banje Beach Club:

- Transport yourself to the tropics at Banje Beach Club, where reggae rhythms and laid-back vibes reign supreme. Nestled on the shores of Banje Beach, this beach club offers a relaxed atmosphere, chilled-out tunes, and a diverse crowd of locals and travelers alike. Whether you're lounging on a sunbed, sipping on a cocktail, or dancing barefoot in the sand, Banje Beach Club is the perfect place to unwind and let your cares drift away on the sea breeze.

Hip Hangout at D'Vino Wine Bar:

- Looking for a more low-key nightlife experience? Head to D'Vino Wine Bar and unwind with a glass of fine wine in a cozy and intimate setting. Located in the heart of Dubrovnik's Old Town, this wine bar offers an extensive selection of Croatian wines, delicious charcuterie boards, and a warm and welcoming atmosphere. So, gather your friends, raise a toast to good times, and savor the flavors of Croatia at this hip hangout.

Dance Floor Delight at Club Lazareti:

- Get ready to dance the night away at Club Lazareti, a legendary nightclub housed in a historic maritime complex. With its underground vibe, eclectic music selection, and lively crowd, Club Lazareti is a favorite among locals and visitors alike. Whether you're into techno, house, or hip-hop, you'll find something to keep you grooving on the dance floor until the early hours of the morning. So, put on your party shoes, let loose, and make memories that will last a lifetime at this iconic Dubrovnik hotspot.

- **Bohemian Vibes at Troubadour Hard Jazz Cafe**:

- Step into the world of live music and intimate gatherings at Troubadour Hard Jazz Cafe. Nestled in the heart of

Dubrovnik's Old Town, this cozy jazz bar offers a laid-back atmosphere and soulful tunes that will transport you to a bygone era. Sip on a classic cocktail, soak in the smooth melodies, and lose yourself in the timeless allure of jazz at this bohemian hotspot.

- **Lively Nights at EastWest Beach Club**:

- Experience the epitome of seaside luxury at EastWest Beach Club, where glamorous vibes and pulsating beats collide. Located on Banje Beach, this upscale beach club offers an opulent setting, plush sunbeds, and a stylish crowd that knows how to party in style. From daytime lounging to late-night revelry, EastWest Beach Club is the perfect place to see and be seen on Dubrovnik's glamorous waterfront.

- **Chic Cocktails at Buža Bar**:

- For a truly unforgettable nightlife experience, head to Buža Bar and watch the sunset over the Adriatic Sea while sipping on a refreshing cocktail. Perched on the cliffs just outside Dubrovnik's city walls, this hidden gem offers stunning views, laid-back vibes, and a sense of serenity that's hard to find elsewhere.

So, grab a seat on the edge of the world, raise a glass to the beauty of nature, and let the magic of Buža Bar cast its spell on you.

- **Eclectic Entertainment at Revelin Club's Terrace**:
- Take your nightlife experience to new heights at Revelin Club's Terrace, where world-class DJs and electrifying performances await. Situated within the walls of a historic fortress, this open-air terrace offers panoramic views of the city and the sea, making it the perfect backdrop for a night of unforgettable entertainment. Dance under the stars, mingle with the crowd, and let the energy of Revelin Club's Terrace sweep you off your feet.
- **Boat Party Bonanza with Dubrovnik Party Boat**:
- Take your nightlife experience to the open sea with a party cruise aboard the Dubrovnik Party Boat. Set sail along the stunning coastline, dance to the latest hits, and sip on cocktails as you soak in the sun and sea breeze. With live DJs, onboard bars, and a lively atmosphere, the Dubrovnik Party Boat is the ultimate floating nightclub experience. So, grab

your swimsuit, hop aboard, and get ready to party like never before on this high seas adventure.

- **Historic Hangout at Troubadour Hard Jazz Cafe**:

- Delve into Dubrovnik's rich history and vibrant nightlife scene at Troubadour Hard Jazz Cafe. Located in a historic building in the heart of the Old Town, this atmospheric jazz bar offers live music, signature cocktails, and a cozy ambiance that's perfect for a night of relaxation and revelry. So, step back in time, unwind with a drink, and let the soothing sounds of jazz transport you to another era at Troubadour Hard Jazz Cafe.

- **Folk Fun at Buža Bar**:

- For a taste of traditional Croatian culture and lively folk music, head to Buža Bar and join in the fun. Situated on the cliffs overlooking the Adriatic Sea, this rustic bar offers a relaxed atmosphere, stunning views, and live performances by local musicians. Sip on a cold beer, tap your feet to the beat, and immerse yourself in the joyous sounds of Croatian folk music at Buža Bar.

Direction

1. **Cave Bar More**:
    - Address: Kardinala Stepinca 33, within the More Hotel, Dubrovnik, Croatia.

2. **Copacabana Beach Club**:
    - Address: Put od Republike 1A, Lapad, Dubrovnik, Croatia.

3. **Culture Club Revelin**:
    - Address: Svačićeva ul. 30, Revelin Fortress, Dubrovnik, Croatia.

4. **Sky Bar**:
    - Address: Lopudska ul. 7, Dubrovnik Hotel, Dubrovnik, Croatia.

5. **Banje Beach Club**:
    - Address: Frana Supila 10, Dubrovnik, Croatia.

6. **Troubadour Hard Jazz Cafe**:
    - Address: Bunićeva poljana 2, Dubrovnik, Croatia.

7. **Revelin Club's Terrace**:
    - Address: Svačićeva ul. 30, Revelin Fortress, Dubrovnik, Croatia.

8. **Dubrovnik Party Boat**:

    - Departure locations may vary; please refer to your booking confirmation for details.

9. **EastWest Beach Club**:

    - Address: Frana Supila 14, Dubrovnik, Croatia.

10. **Buža Bar**:

    - Address: Crijevićeva ul. 9, Dubrovnik, Croatia.

11. **D'Vino Wine Bar**:

    - Address: Palmotićeva ul. 4, Dubrovnik, Croatia.

12. **Club Lazareti**:

    - Address: Frana Supila 14, Lazareti, Dubrovnik, Croatia.

13. **Dubrovnik Hotel (Sky Bar)**:

    - Address: Lopudska ul. 7, Dubrovnik, Croatia.

14. **Banje Beach**:

    - Address: Frana Supila 10, Dubrovnik, Croatia.

10 AMAZING ITENERARIES

et's dive into 10 amazing itineraries to explore the enchanting city of Dubrovnik, each tailored to different preferences and interests!

History Buff's Delight: Step back in time with a journey through Dubrovnik's rich history. Begin by walking the ancient city walls, marveling at the imposing fortifications and panoramic views of the Adriatic Sea. Explore the cobblestone streets of the Old Town, visiting landmarks like the majestic Rector's Palace and the ornate Dubrovnik Cathedral. Dive into the city's past at the Dubrovnik Maritime Museum and the War Photo Limited exhibition, gaining insights into Dubrovnik's maritime heritage and wartime experiences.

Foodie Adventure: Embark on a culinary odyssey through Dubrovnik's gastronomic delights. Start your day with a stroll through the bustling Gundulićeva Poljana Market, sampling local produce and delicacies. Indulge in a seafood feast at one of the waterfront restaurants, savoring fresh catch-of-the-day dishes paired with crisp Croatian wines. Join a cooking class to learn the secrets of Dalmatian cuisine, mastering recipes for seafood risotto, peka, and traditional sweets like rozata. End your day with a sunset cocktail overlooking the shimmering Adriatic Sea.

Island Explorer: Escape the hustle and bustle of the mainland with a day trip to Dubrovnik's nearby islands. Cruise to the idyllic Lokrum Island, home to lush botanical gardens, historic ruins, and peacocks roaming freely. Discover the hidden coves and pristine beaches of the Elafiti Islands, where you can swim, snorkel, and soak up the Mediterranean sun. Enjoy a leisurely lunch at a seaside taverna, feasting on grilled fish and seafood platters before returning to Dubrovnik in time for sunset.

Adventure Seeker's Paradise: Satisfy your thirst for adrenaline with an action-packed day in Dubrovnik's great outdoors. Embark on a thrilling sea kayaking excursion along the rugged coastline, exploring sea caves, hidden beaches, and dramatic cliffs. Strap on your hiking boots and conquer Mount Srđ, rewarded with panoramic vistas of Dubrovnik and the surrounding islands. Take to the skies with a tandem paragliding flight, soaring high above the Adriatic for a bird's-eye view of the stunning landscape.

Art and Culture Trail: Immerse yourself in Dubrovnik's vibrant arts and culture scene. Begin your day with a visit to the Dubrovnik Museum of Modern Art, showcasing works by Croatian and international artists. Wander through the streets of the Old Town, where you'll find numerous galleries and artisan workshops showcasing traditional crafts and contemporary creations. Attend a live performance at the iconic Dubrovnik Summer Festival, featuring opera, theater, and music against the backdrop of historic venues like the Rector's Palace and St. Blaise's Church.

Wellness Retreat: Treat yourself to a day of relaxation and rejuvenation in Dubrovnik's tranquil oasis. Start your morning with a yoga session overlooking the azure waters of the Adriatic Sea, followed by a refreshing swim in the crystal-clear sea. Pamper yourself with a spa day at one of Dubrovnik's luxury resorts, indulging in massages, facials, and holistic treatments inspired by ancient wellness traditions. Unwind with a sunset meditation session atop the city walls, soaking in the peaceful ambiance and panoramic views.

Family Fun Day: Create lasting memories with a day of family-friendly adventures in Dubrovnik. Embark on a treasure hunt through the Old Town, solving riddles and clues to uncover hidden gems and historical landmarks. Spend the afternoon splashing and sliding at the Dubrovnik Aquapark, featuring water slides, pools, and splash zones for all ages. Cap off your day with a sunset cruise around Dubrovnik's coastline, enjoying onboard entertainment and panoramic views of the city's iconic skyline.

Romantic Rendezvous: Celebrate love and romance with a dreamy day in Dubrovnik for couples. Start your morning with a leisurely breakfast at a charming café overlooking the Adriatic Sea, sipping coffee and savoring freshly baked pastries. Take a leisurely stroll through the enchanting gardens of Trsteno Arboretum, where you can admire ancient trees, exotic plants, and stunning sea views. Enjoy a private sunset sailing excursion, toasting to your love with champagne as the sun dips below the horizon.

Nightlife Extravaganza: Experience Dubrovnik's vibrant nightlife scene with an evening of music, dance, and revelry. Begin your night with a pre-dinner cocktail at one of the city's stylish rooftop bars, enjoying panoramic views of the Old Town and Adriatic Sea. Indulge in a gourmet dinner at a trendy restaurant, sampling local specialties and international cuisine. Continue the party at Dubrovnik's hottest clubs and bars, where you can dance the night away to live music, DJ sets, and energetic beats.

Nature Lover's Paradise: Connect with nature's beauty on a day of outdoor exploration in Dubrovnik's pristine landscapes. Start your day with a hike through the lush forests of Mljet National Park, discovering hidden lakes, ancient ruins, and tranquil walking trails. Dive into the crystal-clear waters of the Adriatic Sea for a snorkeling adventure, marveling at colorful coral reefs and marine life. Conclude your day with a sunset picnic on Banje Beach, toasting to the natural wonders of Dubrovnik with local wine and gourmet treats.

48 HOURS IN DUBROVNIK WHAT TO EAT AND DRINK

Day 1:

Morning: Rise and shine, it's time to fuel up for an epic day ahead. Head to a local café like Cogito Coffee or Gradska Kavana Arsenal for a traditional Croatian breakfast of burek, a flaky pastry filled with cheese or meat, accompanied by a strong cup of Croatian coffee. Don't forget to indulge in a slice of krempita, a creamy custard cake, for that extra morning boost.

Mid-morning: After breakfast, take a leisurely stroll through the Old Town and work up an appetite for some mid-morning snacks. Stop by Dubravka 1836 for some homemade pastries or visit a local bakery like Mlinar or Pekara Dubravica for fresh bread and pastries to munch on as you explore the city.

Lunch: When hunger strikes, head to Proto Fish Restaurant for a seafood feast fit for a king. Start with a plate of oysters from nearby Ston, followed by a bowl of brudet, a traditional Croatian fish stew, and finish off with a platter of grilled fish served with a side of blitva, a local Swiss chard dish. Wash it all down with a glass of local white wine or a refreshing lemonade.

Afternoon: After lunch, take a break from eating and explore Dubrovnik's cultural treasures. Visit the

Dubrovnik Cathedral to admire its stunning Baroque architecture, wander through the Rector's Palace to learn about the city's history, and climb to the top of Mount Srđ for panoramic views of the city and surrounding islands.

Dinner: For dinner, treat yourself to a taste of traditional Croatian cuisine at Konoba Dubrava. Start with a plate of pršut, Croatia's answer to prosciutto, served with local cheeses and olives. For your main course, try the pasticada, a slow-cooked beef dish served with gnocchi, followed by a slice of rozata, a creamy custard dessert flavored with rose liqueur.

Evening: End your first day in Dubrovnik with a nightcap at Buža Bar, a hidden gem tucked away in the city walls. Grab a seat on the cliffside terrace, sip on a glass of Croatian wine or a refreshing cocktail, and watch the sun set over the Adriatic Sea. Cheers to a day well spent!

Day 2:

Morning: Start your second day in Dubrovnik with a hearty breakfast at Dubravka 1836. Fuel up with a traditional Croatian breakfast of scrambled eggs, bacon, and grilled tomatoes, served with a side of fresh bread and homemade jam. Wash it all down with a cup of Croatian coffee or a glass of freshly squeezed orange juice.

Mid-morning: After breakfast, take a stroll along the city walls for breathtaking views of the Old Town and the Adriatic Sea. Stop by the Dubrovnik Cable Car and take a ride to the top of Mount Srđ for panoramic views of the city and surrounding islands.

Lunch: For lunch, head to Nautika Restaurant for a fine dining experience overlooking the Adriatic Sea. Start with a plate of octopus salad, followed by a bowl of black risotto made with squid ink and served with a side of grilled vegetables. For your main course, try the grilled sea bass or the lobster pasta, paired with a glass of local white wine.

Afternoon: After lunch, explore Dubrovnik's culinary scene with a visit to the Gundulićeva Poljana Market. Browse the stalls filled with fresh fruits, vegetables, cheeses, and cured meats, and pick up some local specialties to take home as souvenirs.

Dinner: For your final dinner in Dubrovnik, indulge in a tasting menu at 360° Restaurant. Situated on top of the city walls, this Michelin-starred restaurant offers stunning views of the Old Town and the Adriatic Sea. Enjoy a selection of local dishes prepared with fresh, seasonal ingredients, paired with carefully curated wines from Croatia and beyond.

Evening: End your culinary adventure in Dubrovnik with a nightcap at D'Vino Wine Bar.

Choose from a wide selection of Croatian wines, carefully curated by knowledgeable staff, and enjoy a leisurely evening of wine tasting and conversation. Raise a glass to an unforgettable 48 hours in Dubrovnik filled with delicious food and drink!

FESTIVAL AND EVENTS IN DUBROVNIK

1. Dubrovnik Summer Festival:

- Prepare to be dazzled by the Dubrovnik Summer Festival, a month-long extravaganza of music, theater, dance, and art held annually from mid-July to mid-August. The city's historic landmarks serve as stunning backdrops for performances ranging from classical music concerts in open-air venues to Shakespearean plays staged in ancient courtyards. Join the locals and visitors alike as they celebrate the rich cultural heritage of Dubrovnik in this unforgettable summer spectacle.

2. Feast of St. Blaise:

- Experience the magic of the Feast of St. Blaise, the patron saint of Dubrovnik, celebrated each year on February 3rd. This centuries-old tradition honors the city's beloved saint with a colorful procession through the streets of the Old Town, featuring religious ceremonies, live music, and traditional folk dances. Be sure to sample local delicacies like fritule (sweet fritters) and arancini (candied orange peels) as you join in the festivities.

3. Carnival:

- Let loose and embrace your inner reveler at Dubrovnik's Carnival, held in February or March each year in the weeks leading up to Lent. Join costumed locals and visitors as they parade through the streets of the Old Town, accompanied by live music, dancing, and merrymaking. Indulge in traditional carnival treats like krafne (Croatian doughnuts) and kroštule (fried pastries) as you celebrate the arrival of spring with this lively and colorful festival.

4. Dubrovnik International Film Festival:

- Lights, camera, action! Get ready for the Dubrovnik International Film Festival, a showcase of independent cinema from around the world held annually in April. Screenings take place in historic theaters and outdoor venues throughout the city, offering cinephiles the chance to discover new talent and engage in thought-provoking discussions with filmmakers. Don't miss the chance to mingle with industry professionals and fellow film enthusiasts at this dynamic and inspiring event.

5. Dubrovnik Wine & Jazz Festival:

- Sip, swirl, and sway to the smooth sounds of jazz at the Dubrovnik Wine & Jazz Festival, held each year in May. Sample a diverse selection of local wines from the Dubrovnik region as you groove to live performances by world-renowned jazz musicians. With stunning views of the Adriatic Sea as your backdrop, this festival offers the perfect blend of music, wine, and Mediterranean charm.

6. Dubrovnik Winter Festival:

- Embrace the festive spirit at the Dubrovnik Winter Festival, a magical celebration held from late November to early January. The Old Town transforms into a winter wonderland, with twinkling lights, festive decorations, and traditional Christmas markets lining the streets. Enjoy ice skating in the historic square, warm up with mulled wine and roasted chestnuts, and marvel at the stunning holiday displays that light up the city after dark.

7. Dubrovnik Film Festival:

- Lights, camera, Dubrovnik! Experience the glitz and glamour of the Dubrovnik Film Festival, a glamorous showcase of international cinema held annually in October. Rub shoulders with filmmakers, actors, and industry insiders as you attend red carpet premieres, film screenings, and exclusive parties at iconic venues throughout the city. With its stunning setting and star-studded lineup, this festival is a must-attend event for film buffs and cinephiles alike.

8. Dubrovnik Feast of St. Ignatius:

- Join in the festivities of the Feast of St. Ignatius, celebrated each year on July 31st. This religious holiday honors St. Ignatius of Loyola, the founder of the Jesuit order, with a solemn procession through the streets of the Old Town, followed by a spectacular fireworks display over the Adriatic Sea. Experience the beauty and tradition of Dubrovnik's religious heritage as you witness this captivating spectacle.

9. Dubrovnik Maritime Festival:

- Set sail for adventure at the Dubrovnik Maritime Festival, a celebration of the city's rich maritime history held each year in September. Watch as historic sailing ships and traditional galleons glide into the harbor, accompanied by live music, sea shanties, and maritime demonstrations. Explore the bustling waterfront market, sample fresh seafood and local specialties, and immerse yourself in the seafaring traditions of Dubrovnik.

10. Dubrovnik Summer Carnival: - Get ready to party at the Dubrovnik Summer Carnival, a lively celebration held in July and August that brings together locals and visitors of all ages for a week of music, dancing, and fun. Join the colorful parade through the streets of the Old Town, adorned in costumes and masks, and take part in street performances, carnival games, and cultural activities. With its festive atmosphere and joyful energy, the Dubrovnik Summer Carnival is the perfect way to experience the spirit of summer in this enchanting city.

IDEAL VISITING TIME

Ahoy, fellow traveler! Let's set sail on a voyage through the seasons of Dubrovnik, where each month brings its own unique charm and allure.

Spring (March - May):

- Springtime in Dubrovnik is a delightful affair, with mild temperatures and blooming flowers painting the city in vibrant hues. March marks the beginning of the tourist season, with temperatures gradually rising and the streets buzzing with anticipation. April brings warmer weather and longer days, perfect for exploring the city's historic landmarks and scenic landscapes. By May, Dubrovnik is in full bloom, with outdoor cafes and seaside promenades beckoning visitors to bask in the Mediterranean sunshine.

Summer (June - August):

- Ah, summer in Dubrovnik – a time of endless sunshine, azure skies, and bustling streets. June kicks off the peak tourist season, with temperatures soaring into the 80s°F (high 20s°C) and the city's beaches and waterfront cafes teeming with sun-seekers. July and August are the hottest months, with temperatures often reaching the 90s°F (30s°C) and the city's narrow streets and historic sites brimming with visitors. Despite the crowds, summer is the perfect time to soak up the sun, swim in the crystal-clear waters of the Adriatic Sea, and experience the vibrant energy of Dubrovnik's summer festivals and events.

Fall (September - November):

- As summer fades into autumn, Dubrovnik takes on a quieter, more laid-back vibe, making it an ideal time to visit for those seeking a more relaxed experience. September offers warm temperatures and sunny days, perfect for outdoor activities like hiking, sailing, and exploring the city's charming neighborhoods. October brings cooler temperatures and occasional rainfall, but also fewer crowds and lower prices, making it a great time to snag deals on accommodations and activities. By November, Dubrovnik begins to wind down for the winter season, but the city's cultural attractions and historic sites remain open for exploration, offering a more intimate and authentic experience for visitors.

Winter (December - February):

- While winter in Dubrovnik may be cooler and quieter compared to the bustling summer months, it still holds its own special charm for those willing to brave the cooler temperatures. December marks the beginning of the festive season, with Christmas markets, holiday decorations, and seasonal festivities transforming the city into a winter wonderland. January and February are the coldest months, with temperatures dipping into the 40s°F (single digits °C) and occasional snowfall dusting the rooftops of the Old Town. Despite the chill, winter is a magical time to visit Dubrovnik, with fewer tourists, lower prices, and the chance to experience the city's cultural attractions and culinary delights without the crowds.

VOCABULARY AND COMMON PHRASE

Ahoy, language adventurers! Get ready to dive into the linguistic wonders of Dubrovnik with this fun and handy guide to useful phrases and expressions. Whether you're ordering a delicious seafood dish or chatting with the friendly locals, these phrases will help you navigate the city with ease and charm.

1. Greetings and Basics:

- "Dobro jutro!" (DOH-broh YOO-troh!) - Good morning!

- "Dobar dan!" (DOH-bahr dahn!) - Good afternoon!

- "Dobra večer!" (DOH-brah VEH-cher!) - Good evening!

- "Hvala!" (HVAH-lah!) - Thank you!

- "Molim!" (MOH-leem!) - Please!

- "Da" (dah) - Yes

- "Ne" (neh) - No

2. Dining and Food:

- "Jedan stol za jednu osobu, molim." (YEH-dahn stohl zah YEH-dnoo oh-SOH-boo, MOH-leem.) - A table for one, please.

- "Želim naručiti ..." (ZHEH-leem nah-ROO-chee-tee ...) - I would like to order ...
- "Riba" (REE-bah) - Fish
- "Školjke" (SHKOL-yeh) - Shellfish
- "Hobotnica" (hoh-BOHT-nee-tsah) - Octopus
- "Vino" (VEE-noh) - Wine
- "Račun, molim." (RAH-choon, MOH-leem.) - The bill, please.

3. Getting Around:

- "Koliko košta karta?" (KOH-lee-koh KOSH-tah KAHR-tah?) - How much is a ticket?
- "Kuda ide ovaj autobus/tramvaj?" (KOO-dah EE-deh OH-vai OW-vey OW-bus/TRAHM-vai?) - Where does this bus/tram go?
- "Koliko je udaljen/a ...?" (KOH-lee-koh yeh OO-dahl-yen/ah ...?) - How far is ...?
- "Koliko košta taxi do ...?" (KOH-lee-koh KOSH-tah TAHK-see doh ...?) - How much is a taxi to ...?

4. Basic Expressions:

- "Dobrodošli u Dubrovnik!" (DOH-broh-dohsh-lee oo DOO-brohv-neek!) - Welcome to Dubrovnik!

- "Kako se zoveš?" (KAH-koh seh ZOH-vehsh?) - What's your name?

- "Kako si?" (KAH-koh see?) - How are you?

- "Sretan put!" (SREH-tahn poot!) - Have a safe trip!

- "Laku noć!" (LAH-koo nohch!) - Good night!

5. Emergencies:

- "Pomoć!" (POH-mohtch!) - Help!

- "Policija!" (poh-LEE-tsee-yah!) - Police!

- "Hitna pomoć!" (HEET-nah POH-mohtch!) - Emergency!

- "Molim vas, nazovite hitnu pomoć!" (MOH-leem vahs, NAH-zoh-vee-teh HEET-noo POH-mohtch!) - Please call an ambulance!

6. Making Friends:

- "Drago mi je upoznati te!" (DRAH-goh mee yeh ooh-POHZ-nah-tee teh!) - Nice to meet you!

- "Imate li preporuke za dobar restoran?" (ee-MAH-teh lee preh-poh-ROO-keh zah doh-bahr reh-stoh-RAHN?) - Do you have any recommendations for a good restaurant?

- "Jeste li ovdje lokalni?" (YES-teh lee OH-vdyeh LOH-kahl-nee?) - Are you a local here?

- "Možete li mi pokazati put do ...?" (MOH-zheh-teh lee mee poh-KAH-zah-tee poot doh ...?) - Can you show me the way to ...?
- "Zabavljajmo se!" (zah-BAHV-lyahy-moh seh!) - Let's have fun!

7. Shopping and Bargaining:

- "Koliko košta ovo?" (KOH-lee-koh KOSH-tah OH-voh?) - How much does this cost?
- "Mogu li dobiti popust?" (MOH-goo lee DOH-bee-tee POH-poost?) - Can I get a discount?
- "Gdje je najbliža trgovina?" (gd-yeh yeh nai-BLEE-zhah TRGO-vee-nah?) - Where is the nearest store?
- "Imate li ovaj proizvod u drugoj boji/veličini?" (ee-MAH-teh lee OH-vai proh-eez-voht oo droo-goy BOH-yee/veh-LEE-chee-nee?) - Do you have this product in another color/size?

8. Expressing Gratitude:

- "Hvala puno!" (HVAH-lah POO-noh!) - Thank you very much!
- "Hvala lijepa!" (HVAH-lah LEE-yeh-pah!) - Thank you kindly!
- "Hvala na pomoći!" (HVAH-lah nah POH-moh-chee!) - Thank you for your help!

- "Hvala za sve!" (HVAH-lah zah sve!) - Thank you for everything!

9. Beach and Leisure:

- "Gdje je najbliža plaža?" (gd-yeh yeh nai-BLEE-zhah PLAH-zhah?) - Where is the nearest beach?

- "Imate li ležaljke za iznajmljivanje?" (ee-MAH-teh lee LEH-zhahl-kyeh zah eez-NAH-mlyee-vah-nyeh?) - Do you have sunbeds for rent?

- "Mogu li unajmiti suncobran?" (MOH-goo lee oo-NYAH-mee-tee SOON-tsoh-brahn?) - Can I rent a sun umbrella?

10. Cultural Interactions:

- "Kako se kaže ... na hrvatskom?" (KAH-koh seh KAH-zheh ... nah hrvah-TSOH-kohm?) - How do you say ... in Croatian?

- "Što je to?" (shtoh yeh toh?) - What is that?

- "Mogu li fotografirati ovo?" (MOH-goo lee foh-toh-grah-FEE-rah-tee OH-voh?) - Can I take a photo of this?

- "Ovo je predivno!" (OH-voh yeh PREH-deev-noh!) - This is beautiful!

DUBROVNIK TRAVEL PRACTICALITIES

Transportation Options:

- Dubrovnik Airport (DBV) serves as the main gateway to the city, located about 20 minutes from the Old Town.

- Taxis and airport shuttles are readily available for transfers to the city center.

- Public buses run regularly between the airport and Dubrovnik, offering a budget-friendly option for transportation.

- Within the city, walking is often the best way to explore the Old Town and nearby attractions, as many streets are pedestrian-only.

- Local buses and taxis are available for longer journeys or trips to outlying areas.

Local Currency:

- The official currency of Croatia is the Croatian Kuna (HRK).

- Credit cards are widely accepted in hotels, restaurants, and larger stores, but it's always a good idea to carry some cash for smaller purchases and transactions.

Language:

- The official language of Croatia is Croatian, but English is widely spoken, especially in tourist areas like Dubrovnik.
- Learning a few basic phrases in Croatian, such as "hello" (zdravo), "thank you" (hvala), and "please" (molim), can go a long way in making connections with locals.

Recommended Accommodations:

- Dubrovnik offers a range of accommodations to suit every budget and preference, from luxury hotels to budget-friendly hostels and guesthouses.
- For a truly unforgettable experience, consider staying within the walls of the Old Town, where you'll be immersed in the city's rich history and charm.
- Alternatively, accommodations outside the Old Town offer more space and tranquility, with easy access to beaches and other attractions.

Essential Tips:

1. **Sun Protection:** Dubrovnik enjoys plenty of sunshine, so be sure to pack sunscreen, sunglasses, and a hat to protect yourself from the strong Mediterranean sun.

2. **Water:** Stay hydrated, especially during the summer months, by carrying a reusable water bottle with you and refilling it at public fountains or shops.

3. **Comfortable Shoes:** With its cobblestone streets and steep staircases, Dubrovnik can be challenging to navigate in high heels or sandals. Opt for comfortable walking shoes to explore the city with ease.

4. **Reservations:** During peak tourist season, it's advisable to book accommodations, tours, and restaurant reservations in advance to avoid disappointment and ensure availability.

5. **Respect Local Customs:** Dubrovnik is a conservative city with strong Catholic traditions, so dress modestly when visiting churches or religious sites, and avoid loud or disruptive behavior in public spaces.

CONCLUSION

As the sun sets over the shimmering Adriatic Sea and the ancient walls of Dubrovnik cast long shadows across the cobblestone streets, it's time to bid farewell to our journey through the Dubrovnik Travel Guide 2024. From the historic streets of Dubrovnik Old Town to the serene shores of Lapad, from the bustling port of Gruž to the tranquil neighborhoods of Mokošica, we've explored every corner of this enchanting city together.

Through the pages of this comprehensive handbook, you've navigated the labyrinthine alleys of Dubrovnik's Old Town, discovered hidden gems and must-see attractions, and indulged in the flavors of local delights that tantalize the taste buds and warm the soul. You've walked in the footsteps of ancient civilizations, marveled at architectural wonders, and forged unforgettable memories against the backdrop of Croatia's gem.

But beyond the practical tips and insider insights, it's the moments of wonder, joy, and connection that truly define the essence of travel. It's the laughter shared over a glass of local wine, the awe inspired by panoramic views of the Adriatic, and the warmth of hospitality extended by locals eager to share their stories and traditions.

As you close the pages of this guide and reflect on the experiences shared within, may you carry with you the spirit of Dubrovnik – a city of beauty, history, and endless possibilities. And as you journey onward, may you continue to explore, discover, and embrace the magic of travel wherever your adventures may take you.

From the depths of our hearts, we extend a heartfelt thank you for choosing the Dubrovnik Travel Guide 2024 as your companion on this unforgettable journey. May your travels be filled with wonder, your memories be cherished, and may Dubrovnik forever hold a special place in your heart.

Until we meet again on the shores of the Adriatic, farewell, dear traveler, and may the spirit of Dubrovnik guide you on your next great adventure.

Printed in Great Britain
by Amazon